The
Elsie & Pooka
Wheel of the Year Stories
- Winter -

Written and illustrated by
Lora Craig-Gaddis

Published by The Pie Plate Publishing Co.
P.O. Box 760151
Lathrup Village, MI 48076
www.pieplatepublishing.com

The Pie Plate Publishing Co.

(Softcover Edition) ISBN: 978-1-941175-90-3

1 2 3 4 5 6 7 8 9 10

Original Cover Art & Interior Illustration by Lora Gaddis
Layout and Design by Steve Czapiewski.

Please contact the publisher about bulk and educational discounts on this book.

In Memory of My Teachers:

my Mother, my Grandmother, the Great-Aunts
and Judith DeFrain.

Introduction

Meet Elsie and Pooka: Elsie is a young witch and herbalist. Her best friend and familiar is Pooka, a small mischievous black cat. Together, they will help guide your child through the year's Wheel of Pagan Holidays.

Through these pages, children will be taught by Elsie and learn along with Pooka. Elsie, with her patience and gentle wisdom, provides a positive role model and instructor while children identify with Pooka, the little cat. He asks questions. He makes them laugh. Sometimes he even gets into trouble. They learn as he learns.

Perhaps, Pooka is the magical child in all of us…

Lora Craig-Gaddis

P.S. Besides the colored illustrations, this book contains many line drawings. Your child has Pooka's permission to color all of them!

Pooka

Contents

Yule

Imbolc

Market Day

Yule

Yule is celebrated on the Winter Solstice and is actually a birthday party for the sun! At Yule, the sun is "born" once more, and gets a little stronger and stays in the sky a little longer each day after that.

Pagans celebrate the sun's birth much as Christians celebrate Christmas. In fact, most Christmas customs and symbols came from Pagan Yule traditions. Lights and candles, feasting, singing and presents, decorating the house with evergreens and mistletoe, and gathering together with family & friends are all a traditional part of this joyous celebration.

Pooka's Yule Present

Pooka sat on the ledge of the window in Elsie's herb room. Through the panes of leaded glass he stared gloomily out at the snow piling higher and higher, blanketing the whole garden and the forest beyond. He was thoroughly miserable.

In the corner of the herb room crackled a cheery fire on the tiny stone hearth where he could have been warm and toasty. Pooka preferred to be miserable.

"I want to go outside," he wailed.

Behind him, Elsie glanced up from the pomander she was making. A little smile twitched at her mouth.

"So, go."

The cat glared at her. His witch said the most ridiculous things sometimes! She knew very well that it was cold and wet out there and that it had been for weeks!

He stood up and stalked out of the room.

He wandered into the parlor and spotted the Yule tree standing proudly majestic on the far side of the room. He, Elsie, and Edgar, the crow, had trimmed it a few nights ago with shiny brass suns and polished silver moons, gingerbread cookie pentagrams and gilded acorns then draped it with garlands of popcorn and cranberries laced over and under the fragrant branches. At the time, Elsie had told him he mustn't sharpen his claws on the trunk. But she'd never said *why*.

So, Pooka strolled over to the tree and proceeded to do just that. His claws dug in and pulled. It felt so good! The tree wobbled precariously in its pot and the ornaments danced in the loveliest way. Pooka, his troubles forgotten for the moment …or perhaps from a sense of pure orneriness…clawed even deeper, watching the ornaments swing and sway above him. Suddenly they loomed very large, rushing toward him! He sprang out of the way as the tree tipped and crashed to floor.

Pooka dove under Elsie's "reading" chair by the hearth, his little black nose just barely poking out from under the ruffled bottom. He felt her hurried approach and then her boots stopped inches from his nose.

He held his breath – then peeked up through the ruffle. Yup, she was mad! Fists planted on her hips, she scowled down at him. The little cat peered up at her and tried to look innocent. "Edgar did it?"

"Pooka!"

He retreated further under the chair and flattened his ears.

"Well, it's the only tree around … and you won't let me claw the furniture!" he growled.

Elsie sighed and pulled the tree upright again. Then she began replacing the ornaments.

The next morning, Pooka burrowed his way out from under the quilt on Elsie's bed and sprang to the window. Outside the world was still white, the sky was a gloomy gray and the sun was just a feeble rosy spot in the sky. His breath made a moist fog on the inside of the glass. The little cat's whiskers drooped as he turned away. He felt very depressed.

He wound his body around her ankles in desperation as she tried to dress. "Elsie, you're a witch. Make the sun come back!" he pleaded.

She leaned over and picked him up, cuddling him and scratching in all the right places.

But Pooka's purring stopped when she told him, "I can't. This is up to the Goddess. She'll give birth to the sun when it's time."

When would that be? Pooka wondered. It seemed like it had been cold and dark forever! Just thinking about it, he shivered.

Elsie went downstairs and lit the fire in her little stove. Soon the cheery kitchen warmed and the cottage smelled of cinnamon and fresh baked rolls with icing. Pooka curled up in the pillow on the rocking chair and watched Elsie feed Edgar his bits of breakfast. The crow cawed, "More, more," and opened his beak wide, but Pooka knew Edgar would stash at least half of what he got around the kitchen in order to retrieve it later.

"Why are you feeding him so much?" he asked. "Won't we run out of food? What if Winter never ends?"

"No, we won't run out. And, of course, Winter will end, silly!" smiled Elsie. "But, while it's cold out, critters like Edgar need an extra layer on their bodies to stay warm."

"Where's my extra?" Pooka demanded.

Elsie raised one eyebrow. "If you aren't going outside, you don't need it!"

Pooka scowled at her.

But he cheered up later when Elsie poured eggnog for each of them and pulled out all the lovely things she'd been baking the past week. Candles and lamps glowed throughout the cottage and a specially decorated oak log was laid on the hearth. Elsie lit incense and the tall golden Yule candle wreathed in holly. She strummed on her little mandolin and sang songs with Edgar cawing along. Pooka laughed at them both and buried his head under a pillow.

And there were Presents! Elsie laughed and clapped her hands as Edgar and Pooka excitedly ripped open the brightly covered packages. Soon, Edgar was stashing and retrieving the assortment of shiny baubles the witch had made for him. Elsie cuddled in her chair by the fire, her nose buried in a book from Aunt Tilly as Pooka played with his new catnip mouse. For some reason he felt deliriously happy batting it about and pouncing on it, even after one button eye was missing and its tail was soaked with kitty drool.

It was very late when Edgar was finally snoozing on his perch in the kitchen and the cat and his witch trundled up to bed.

Pooka purred as he burrowed under the quilt to tuck himself behind Elsie's knees. It had been a wonderful, magical night!

Hours later, the house was very dark and very quiet when Pooka felt Elsie climb out of bed. Sleepily, he watched her dress and head down to the kitchen.

In a short while, she came back upstairs and got him. "I have something to show you," she said.

Wrapping herself in a thick hooded cloak, she bundled the cat in a small blanket and stuffed him in a basket along with a thermos and some Yule cakes. With another, larger quilt slung over her shoulder, they headed outside where the stars above sparked like tiny jewels through the crisp cold air and the snow crunched under her feet like potato chips.

"Where are we going?" asked Pooka.

"You'll see," answered the little witch mysteriously.

She headed for their special hill that overlooked the forest. She spread the thick quilt on the ground and they sat down, still wrapped in their blankets. Elsie poured warm sweet milk laced with anise & maple into a pair of mugs. Pooka stuck his nose out of the quilt and lapped his up eagerly. He couldn't help purring as his tummy warmed and the only chill that reached him was the frosty air coming through his little black nose.

"What are we doing?"

Elsie sipped from her mug and told him, "We're waiting."

"For what?"

"You'll see."

So Pooka waited. Within a few moments, the forest was bathed in a faint golden light and the sky became a rosy pink and blue. And peeking over the tops of the hills and trees was the loveliest orb of rose and gold light.

Pooka's eyes widened, miniature mirrors of what was before him. "What is it?" he whispered.

"It's the sun," Elsie whispered back. "It's the newborn baby sun."

"Will the snow go away now?" Pooka asked eagerly.

"No," she told him. "The sun's still newly born and weak; it must grow stronger. But each day now will last a little bit longer. And before too very long, all the snow will be gone and you'll be outside playing again."

To Pooka, huddled in his blanket, this all still seemed to be a long time off. But at least it was Beginning! He marveled at the magic of the baby sun being born and felt that, somehow, this was the best Yule present of all!

THE LITTLE KITCHEN WITCH

Elsie's Most Excellent Gingerbread Hot Cocoa

The perfect thing to warm you up on a frosty Yule morning ... from your tummy to your toes!

In a heavy saucepan, whisk together :

3 egg yolks
3 ½ cups of whole milk
¾ cup of sugar
1 tsp. cinnamon
1 ½ tsp. powdered ginger
½ tsp. powdered cloves
1/8 tsp. salt

Turn the fire on to a medium heat and cook it for about 10 minutes, stirring the whole time, until the mixture starts getting thicker. Make sure it does not boil and that you stir all the way to the bottom of the pot.

Once it begins to thicken, turn the fire down to the lowest it will go and add 1 cup of finely chopped white chocolate baking bars. Keep cooking it on low, stirring it the whole time, until the chocolate has melted. Then stir in ½ teaspoon of vanilla and ladle it into mugs. Top with a dollop of whipped cream and a sprinkle of cinnamon. Miniature marshmallows are optional...but decadently delicious!

Makes enough for 4 people or one Pooka.

Magic Fudge

Here is a foolproof fudge recipe that even the smallest witch can make:

In a glass bowl, combine 2 cups of semi-sweet chocolate chips and a 14 oz. can of sweetened condensed milk. Microwave it on high for 1 minute. Stir it. Microwave it for another minute. Stir it. Microwave it again for a minute. Now keep stirring til the chips are melted and it's nice and smooth.

Stir in 1 teaspoon of vanilla extract and, if you like nuts, add about 1 cup of chopped walnuts.

Dump the whole thing into an 8-inch square pan lined with tin foil and stick it in the fridge for about 2 hours. Then, cut it into pieces and try not to eat it all at once!

You can also make butterscotch fudge using butterscotch chips or vanilla fudge using white chocolate chips. Sometimes, instead of nuts, Elsie likes to use little bits of smashed peppermint candy canes in the fudge.

Pooka's Winter Cold

Pooka huddled close to the fire on the hearth. Too close. In fact, he could sense the ends of his whiskers singeing…but the cat didn't care. He was chilled and shivering. His eyes watered, his fur was spiky, he ached all over, his nose was hot and besides that……ACHOO! He sneezed so hard that he almost fell off the hearth.

The door of the cottage swung open and Elsie bustled in, her arms filled with packages from shopping. She stomped the snow from her boots, set down her packages and hung up her cloak on a peg. Only then did she notice the miserable little black ball of fur.

The witch rushed over, her cheeks rosy red from the cold and her eyes dark with concern. "Pooks! What is it?" She ran her hands over the cat, feeling his nose and footpads, peering in his eyes.

Pooka moaned pitifully. "Elsie, I'm dying!" and then he sneezed again.

The corners of Elsie's mouth twitched as she suppressed a grin. "You're not dying, Pooka. You just have a cold!"

Glassy amber eyes glared at her. "Easy for YOU to say!"

The girl dropped a kiss on his head. "I'll make you some chicken soup," she said.

Pooka's ears swiveled forward. Hot chicken soup sounded pretty good but …"Elsie, don't you have some herbs or something that will make me better?"

She smiled. "Yes. Oregano, thyme, garlic and onion. And they all go in the soup."

"Oh. Okay." He closed his eyes again.

Before long, Pooka was settled down on a soft green pillow in a basket on the hearth, a steaming bowl of soup in front of him. He lapped up the broth, ate a few of the noodles and chicken bits and left the carrots and celery. He felt a bit better, but still far from well.

His gaze fell on the brightly lit Yule tree in the corner of the parlor. Thinking to cheer himself up, he got out of the basket and stretched his aching muscles. He then slowly made his way over it. He sniffed through the pile of wrapped gifts scattered underneath it. Nothing! He sniffed them all over once again.

"Elsie! My catnip mouse isn't here! You didn't forget it this year, did you?"

The witch looked up from her chair by the fire and laid her book in her lap. "It's there. You just can't smell it."

"But that's dumb! I can always smell catnip - no matter how good you hide it!"

"Well, not this year, " she grinned. "You have a cold, remember?"

Pooka thought about this. He suddenly realized that all the familiar smells of Yule were missing! He couldn't detect the pine fragrance of the tree or the gingerbread cookies in the oven or even the spiced cider that Elsie was sipping. This was Awful!

He slunk back over to his basket and hunkered down again.

Elsie looked sympathetic. "I'll go get you some more soup," she said.

As soon as she left, Edgar the crow flew down from his winter perch on the bookshelves. He snagged an end of the popcorn garland draped on the tree and hopped over to Pooka, the strand trailing behind him. "Wanna play?"

Pooka sneezed on him.

"Ahck!" Edgar jumped back, wings flapping. He dropped the popcorn and flew back up to his perch where he could scold Pooka from a safer distance.

Elsie walked in and frowned. "Pooka, how many times do I have to tell you – leave the ornaments on the tree!" She picked up the garland and carefully replaced it. Pooka felt too miserable to explain that he hadn't done it. He closed his eyes again.

Elsie set the bowl down in front of him and sat on the hearth stroking his fur.

"I'm going to miss Yule, aren't I?" sighed the little cat.

"Oh no, Pooks. You'll be well by then, I'm sure!"

But the thought of not being able to go out and see the Yule sun rise or enjoy his new catnip mouse was just too depressing for Pooka. He closed his eyes and soon was fast asleep.

A little while later, he woke and sniffed the air. He could smell something! What was it?

He looked around and there, not far from him on the hearth, was a pot of simmering eucalyptus leaves. He could smell it!

Elsie smiled at him. "I thought that might help a bit."

Pooka went over and stuck his nose right in the pot, letting the fragrant steam roll over him. He inhaled deeply. This set off another sneezing attack, but he didn't care. He could breathe! He could smell!

By Yule Eve, he felt better yet. He even felt well enough to join Edgar in pulling the popcorn garlands off the Yule tree. They both got in trouble this time!

He still couldn't quite pick out which wrapped gift under the tree held his catnip mouse, but he could smell that it was there somewhere! He could also enjoy the aroma of the wonderful chicken soup that Elsie kept bringing him and the spicy orange fragrance of the bowl of pomanders that she had set on the table.

The evening was filled with merriment and goodies! They lit a special candle for the sun. Elsie brought out her little banjo mandolin and insisted on singing Yule carols. Edgar and Pooka ran and hid in laughing protest as the witch's clear voice persisted in hitting all the wrong notes! Later, they had eggnog and gingerbread next to the special Yule log blazing in the fire. Elsie told them about how, now that the sun was being born again, it would stay a bit longer in the sky each day until the earth warmed up and it would be Spring once more.

Finally, the girl hung a stocking for each of them on the mantle and they went to bed. It was cold upstairs, so Pooka crawled under the covers and curled up behind Elsie's knees.

He couldn't wait for her to wake him early, before dawn, so they could watch the sun rise. It was a ritual they enjoyed every year.

But when he woke and crawled out from the nice warm spot where he'd been sleeping, the sun was already coming up!

"Elsie! Wake up!" The cat leaped on the sleeping witch's chest and patted her warm cheek with his paw. "We're missing it!"

Elsie peeked at him through squinty, glassy eyes – and then sneezed! Pooka jumped out of the way and looked at her in astonishment. Then he noted the bright pink spots on her cheeks and nose before she rolled over back into her pillow. "Go 'way," she muttered.

"Uh oh, I think you have a cold!"

She coughed and batted him away feebly with one hand.

"Poor Elsie!" cried Pooka. "Hang on! I'll go make chicken soup. I'll simmer some Eucalyptus for you too so you can smell the catnip!"

He bounded down the stairs and galloped into the kitchen. Suddenly, he skidded to a stop and looked down in dismay at his front paws. No thumbs!

"Oh, dear," he muttered, then called over his shoulder, "Elsie? I may need a little help here…?"

Elsie's HERB GARDEN

Fragrant Herbal Gifts to Make

Spice beads are great fun to create and their fragrance lasts many years.

Mix about 2 tablespoons of tragacanth gum (available from herb shops or on-line) with about 2 or 3 tablespoons of a fragrant oil such as cinnamon, rose or lavender and about 1 ½ cups of water. Stir it all together til it's nice and slimy.

Then add about 1 cup of combined powdered cinnamon, cloves, lavender and orrisroot.

Mix this all up. It should be about the same consistency as when you make mud pies.

Now, roll it into little beads (about ¼ inch diameter) and set them somewhere to dry for about a day. When they're partly dry, use a big needle and some thread and string the beads into a necklace. Hang them somewhere and let them dry completely. This may take a couple more days. Move them around on the string from time to time as they dry to keep them from sticking.

Your body heat from wearing them or handling them will release a wonderful fragrance.

People love to get these as gifts! To make them extra pretty, you can alternate the spice beads with other, more conventional types of beads on the strand.

Pomanders have been a traditional decoration and gift at Yule for hundreds of years. People would give each other clove-studded oranges as a magic symbol of prosperity for the coming year. You can also hang them from your tree or set several of them out in a pretty bowl to make a room smell nice.

The first thing you do is make up a batch of spice mixture. For this, you will need to combine about:

4 ounces of powdered cinnamon
2 ounces of powdered cloves
½ ounce of powdered allspice
½ ounce of powdered nutmeg
1 ounce of powdered orrisroot

People sometimes add lavender buds to the mixture as well. This formula will make enough to do several pomanders.

For the pomanders themselves, you can use oranges, lemons or limes.

Take the fruit and use a nail to pierce the skin and insert a whole clove. Using a nail first to make the hole will keep you from having sore fingers by the time you're finished.

Cover the whole fruit with cloves (it will last almost indefinitely this way) or you can make designs such as spirals, pentacles or sun patterns.

When you've finished studding them with the cloves, pour half of your spice mixture into a bowl large enough to hold your pomanders. Put the pomanders in the bowl and cover them with the other half of the spice mixture.

Leave them in the spices for about a week, turning the pomanders each day. After a week, tie a pretty ribbon around them and hang them in a warm, ventilated place to dry until they're hardened and shriveled. You could even, at this point, hang them on your Yule tree! They will smell wonderful and keep their fragrance for a long time.

If the scent starts to fade after a while, dunk the pomanders quickly in a bowl of warm water and then leave them in the spice mixture again for a week.

Another fun way to use pomanders is to stick the cloves in an orange creating a pattern – don't cover the whole thing – and then float them in a bowl of Yuletide punch for a unique and flavorful decoration.

Potpourri Gel Jars are another gift you can make, and depending on the fragrance you choose, even boys and men will like them.

You will need:

Jars with lids (small mason jars for canning are perfect but you can also use leftover jars from baby food, applesauce or whatever)
2 cups of distilled water
4 packages of plain Gelatin (like Knox gelatin from the grocery store)
50 drops of fragrance oil (any scent you like)
food coloring (any color)

Stir the gelatin into 1 cup of cold water til it dissolves. Then add a cup of very hot water with the food coloring added.

Put some of the oil into each of your jars (how much you use depends on the size of the jar. For a baby food jar, use about 10 drops)

If you want, and your jar is large enough, you can also put in a couple of cinnamon sticks or dried flowers to make it extra pretty.

Then pour in the gelatin mixture in the jars and put them in the refrigerator for a couple of hours. After that, you can store them at room temperature with their lids on.

To release the fragrance, just take off the lids.

The jar lids can be decorated with fabric, ribbon, raffia, and sprigs of holly or evergreen.

Pooka Says: Don't forget that kitties like presents too! Put some dried catnip in a jar and use it to store your cat's favorite toys. Every time you pull one out, it will have the catnip scent that makes your fur-person go wild! When the toy starts to loose its fragrance, just drop it back in the jar for a few days.

A Present for Elsie

The first frost had arrived, coating all the twigs and leaves in the forest with sparkling icy edges. Pooka's paws were cold and, as he padded along the path toward the stream, he stopped occasionally to shake one of them. He wished he'd remembered to wear the paw-covers that Elsie had made for him last Yule – but he'd been in too much of a hurry to leave the cottage.

The cat sighed, his warm breath making little white puffs in the cold air. Elsie sometimes let him play with balls of yarn. How was he supposed to know that the other end of that particular ball of purple yarn was attached to a sweater she was making for Aunt Tilly? And, besides, he grumbled, what was the big deal? She still had a few days before Yule to fix the parts that he'd unraveled!

Pooka wondered how to amuse himself until it was safe to return to the cottage. He'd reached the stream and spotted a fallen tree trunk extending into the water. A graceful bound landed him on top of the trunk and he trotted along its length till he reached the end. There he sat and gazed at the little silver minnows darting around below him. As Pooka studied the fish, his ears suddenly pricked forward and his whiskers sprang to attention. What was that?

He hunkered down on his belly and leaned over the log, peering closely now into the water.

"Rawk! Don't fall in!" croaked a voice in his ear, and the startled cat jumped and scrambled and almost did end up in the water!

"Edgar! Don't sneak up on me like that!" Pooka yelled as he dug his claws into the wood.

The crow looked offended. "I didn't sneak. I flew. I landed. You just didn't hear me. What were you doing?"

"I saw something in the water," said Pooka.

"Fish?" asked Edgar.

"No. I mean, yes, there were fish. But something else too. Something long and sort of greenish gold."

Spreading his great black wings for balance, the bird craned his neck out and studied the water carefully.

Pooka said, "There. On the bottom around those rocks."

After a long moment, Edgar straightened up and folded his wings back in. "It's a sparkly," he announced. "A people sparkly. The neck kind."

"You mean a necklace?" asked Pooka.

The bird dipped his head. "Yup. With a roundy thingy on it," he added.

Pooka peered into the water again. Edgar was right! It did look as though there was some sort of medallion on the chain.

"How do we get it out?" he asked.

"Get what out?" piped up a third voice. Glancing over his shoulder, Pooka saw Thistle landing delicately on the edge of the log.

"Pooka found a sparkly," Edgar told her.

"Where?" she asked.

"In the water. At the bottom."

The little fairy took to the air again and hovered inches above the stream, studying it closely. "Those stupid fish are in the way!" she pouted.

Pooka leaned over as far as he dared and batted the water with his paw. Brrrr! It was cold! But his action frightened the fish into scattering.

"I see it! I see it!" cried Thistle excitedly. "Oh, Pooks! Can I have it? Please? I'll be your friend!"

Pooka blinked his eyes at her slowly. "You already ARE my friend," he reminded the fairy. "Besides, how are we going to get it out of the water?"

The three of them pondered this for a few minutes.

Thistle snapped her fingers. "I've got it!! Edgar, you grab Pooka's tail in your beak and hang on really tight. We'll dangle Pooka into the water and he can grab the sparkly with his claws!" She smiled proudly at the Cleverness of this Idea.

Edgar and Pooka just stared at her for a moment. Finally Pooka exploded. "Are you out of your itsy bitsy mind? That water's COLD! And even if it wasn't, Cats Don't Do Water!" He growled for emphasis.

Thistle's smile faded. She gave a shrug. "Okay, so there are a few details to be worked out. Does anyone have a better plan?"

The three of them looked at each other and then gazed at the water in glum silence.

Just then, a dark haired boy came sauntering along the trail behind them. He carried a long pole over his shoulder and a basket under one arm. "Hey, what's all the racket? You're going to scare the fish away!"

"Caar-Caar-Kaw!" cried Edgar flapping his wings.

"Nathan!" cried Pooka and Thistle. They all started talking at once.

"Pooka found a sparkly," said Thistle. "He's going to give it to me,"

"No I'm not," said Pooka.

"Kraw!" said Edgar.

Thistle said, "It's in the water."

"She wants Edgar to dangle me in the water by my tail!" said Pooka.

"Rawk!" said Edgar - which is crow talk for "dumb fairy". Nathan didn't speak crow. Thistle, however, understood perfectly. She planted her tiny fists on her hips and glared at the bird. "It was a perfectly good idea!" she insisted.

"Nathan, it looks like a medallion on a chain. I want to give it to Elsie, but I don't know how to get it out!"

The fairy looked at Pooka in astonishment. "You're not going to give it to me?"

"I'm sorry, Thistle," Pooka said. "But it's almost Yule. And every Yule Elsie gives me a present. Just once, I'd like to have something to give her."

"Oh," said the fairy. She nodded. "I know what you mean."

"Hmmm…." Nathan set his basket down on the bank of the stream. Placing one foot before the other, he carefully balanced his way out to the end of the log. He brushed his bangs away from his eyes and peered down.

"I see it," he said. The boy reached out over the water with his fishing pole and lowered the line. He made several attempts to snag the chain with his hook, but the movement of the stream kept sweeping the line past it. "Thistle," he said. "Fly out over the stream, grab that line and see if you can position it so it floats into the chain instead of around it."

Little Thistle darted out and, after a couple of tries, announced: "I got it!"

Nathan slowly raised the fishing line. Pooka held his breath once when it got snagged on some rocks, but Thistle managed to wiggle it free without loosing the medallion. Nathan pulled the line out of the water and grabbed the medallion. Everyone cheered. Then they all gathered around on the bank of the stream to have a look.

Finally, Pooka said, "I don't know if Elsie would want it. It's kind of cruddy and lumpy." And indeed, although glints of gold shone through here and there, for the most part the chain and the medallion were covered with a thick brownish green crust. Even Edgar looked disappointed.

Nathan picked at the crust with his fingernail and some of it flaked off. "You know what?" he said. "That's just from being in the water a real long time. My grandmother has something that will get it off. I'll be right back!" The boy took off at a run down the path and, before long, was back with bottle of liquid. When he pulled the cork out, Thistle shot straight up in the air like a tiny rocket. "Pheeuoo!" she exclaimed. "That stuff stinks!"

Pooka backed up and wrinkled his nose. "It smells like vinegar!"

"It is!" grinned Nathan. He put the medallion and chain into a little dish that he'd also brought and poured the vinegar over it. "Now we let it sit for a few minutes to loosen the crud and then we should be able to scrub it right off."

It actually took more than a few minutes but as the cruddy deposits loosened, Edgar chipped off the larger chunks with his beak, Nathan polished the flat parts and Thistle attacked the tiny crevices. Pooka watched and wished there was a way HE could help.

When they were finally done, they sat back and admired the results of their labor. For the first time, the design on the medallion was revealed and Pooka gasped. "It's a sun!" - for so it was – an intricately detailed little sun of shiny gold.

"It's perfect for Yule because that's the birthday of the sun!" cried Pooka. "Elsie's going to love it!"

The friends all sat around grinning at each other and feeling very proud of themselves.

But then a thought occurred to Pooka. "I never could have gotten it out of the water or polished it up without help. I think it should be from ALL of us!"

Nathan, Edgar and Thistle were delighted with this idea for they too had been stumped on what to give the little witch for Yule.

Thistle clapped her hands together. "We'll need to wrap it up all special and pretty for her!"

Nathan thought he could find a suitable box somewhere; Edgar said that he had a bit of shiny gold foil paper to wrap it in; and Pooka, with a mischievous glint in his eye, said he just MIGHT be able to come up with some purple yarn for a bow!

WitchCrafts

A Yule Tree for the Birds

Every year during the Yule Season, Elsie and Pooka decorate a special tree outside with edible ornaments for the birds. Because he is a cat, Pooka has to be persuaded not to chase the birds that come to feast, but he still enjoys watching them.

First, Elsie gathers cranberries, chunks of dried fruit, stale popcorn, peanuts still in their shells and raisins. Then she takes a large needle and some stout thread and strings it all into long garlands.

After that, she takes pinecones and spreads peanut butter into the crevices, then rolls them in a bowl of birdseed. She ties a bright red ribbon around the top to form a loop to hang them with.

Oranges are halved, some of the inside is scooped out and into the hollow she spoons some suet or peanut butter mixed with sunflower seeds. Again, ribbons are poked through the top for hanging.

Stale doughnuts, especially the kinds with colorful sprinkles, also make pretty decorations – and the birds love them!

When all the decorations are ready, the little witch and her cat go outside and drape the garlands along the branches of the tree and hang the ornaments using the loops of ribbon. She even ties whole red and green apples and small cobs of yellow corn with ribbon and adds those. When they are finished, it looks beautiful and the birds enjoy a very happy Yule!

Sometimes, Elsie will decorate a Yule wreath with these goodies and hang that out also. Then, she and Pooka will go inside to sit by a window and count all the different kinds of birds that come to the Winter Feast.

A Fairy Merry Yuletide

As Elsie lit the Yule candle in the window and banked the fire in the hearth, Pooka gave their parlor one last lingering look. All around he could see the remnants of their wonderful evening. Beneath the little fir tree they'd decorated, piles of colorfully wrapped packages beckoned. One of them, he knew, held a catnip mouse!

Pooka wasn't ready for the evening to end.

"Maybe we could open just one present tonight?" he begged.

"No," said the witch firmly. "We're going to wait until morning when the others get here. Besides, I know which one you'll pick and then you'll be up all night playing with it! You won't get a wink of sleep."

"But Elsie, I'm not tired!" he protested.

"I am," she yawned. "Come on, Pooks. It's bedtime and we want to get up extra early to greet the newborn sun!"

He sighed and followed her slowly upstairs. The witch was already in bed when he got there. They shared a mug of warm eggnog and then Elsie blew out the bedside candle.

Pooka curled up next to her and tried very hard to get sleepy. A little while later, Elsie was snoring softly but the cat was still wide-awake.

Suddenly, there came a tap at the window. He lifted his head and, silhouetted against the moonlight, a tiny figure with iridescent wings was hovering just outside.

In a flash, Pooka was at the window and pushing it open with his paw.

"Thistle?"

"Come on!" the fairy whispered.

"Where are we going?"

"To the Forest!"

Pooka didn't need to be asked twice, but just then Elsie in her sleep gave a snort. He froze, but she rolled over and resumed snoring. Hurriedly, the little cat grabbed his hat and launched himself onto a branch of the old apple tree next to the window. He began scrambling down the trunk but halfway his claws lost their grip and he landed in a snowdrift. He shook the icy particles from his fur and whiskers and looked around for Thistle.

The pixie was already beyond the garden gate and past the bridge of the little stream that separated Elsie's cottage from the rest of the forest.

"Come ON!" she urged. Pooka galloped after her.

The glittering stars overhead disappeared as they entered the canopy of trees and the forest seemed very dark. Even with his kitty night-vision, it was hard to see where he was going. He had only the faint glowing ball of light that surrounded the fairy to guide him. Thistle, in her haste, kept darting ahead, around bends and past trees, at times disappearing all together!

"Wait up!" he called. The pixie reappeared in front of him, grabbed his whiskers and tugged him forward. "Hurry! We'll miss all the Fun!"

"Ouch!" Pooka shook his head. Thistle lost her hold on his whiskers and went tumbling into a snow bank.

"What fun? What's going on?"

The little sprite sat in the snow and grinned at him.

"The Fairies' Yule Celebrations, you Big Silly! We have them every year, but You were always Sleeping!"

Pooka blinked at her in surprise. "Fairies celebrate Yule?" he asked. Somehow, the thought had never occurred to him.

Thistle rolled her eyes. "Duh! All of Nature celebrates the sun's rebirth!" She jumped up. "Now Hurry or we'll Miss It!"

"A Fairy Celebration!" exclaimed Pooka. "Well, what are we waiting for?"

It didn't take them long to reach Elsie's Meadow at the edge of the forest. The grove of pine trees that crowned the little hill on the far side of the meadow glowed against the darkness with a faint, shimmering, golden light. At first, Pooka thought the sun was already rising. Then he realized that the light was the result of many fairies gathered together.

"Come on, Pooka!" cried Thistle soaring ahead of him again.

Panting, he reached the top of the hill and the trees. He was instantly greeted by a tiny snowball in his face – it hit him smack between the eyes! Before he could recover, fairies and elves surrounded him.

"It's Pooka!"

"Hey, look who's awake this year!"

One of the fairies tugged playfully on his ear. "Yeah, you old Sleepy Head!"

A dark haired fairy kissed his nose. "We're glad you could join us, WitchCat!" said Berry.

"I brought him!" Thistle reminded the others, lest they forget HER Important Role.

In a show of proper respect, they pelted her with snowballs till the pixie was forced to dive for cover. This, of course, led to lots of giggling and a flurry of teensy snowballs flying in every direction!

Pooka wanted to play – but how can a kitty throw snowballs? He spotted a small snowman (probably made by one of the elves). Taking aim, he batted it with his paw. The head of the snowman whizzed through the air and caught one of them in the chest. The size and force of the ball of snow flattened the little elf. He lay on his back, very still. The other elves and fairies held their breath. After a few moments, he sat up slowly and shook his head. Berry rushed to his side. "Bracken! Are you okay?" The elf responded with a lopsided grin. "Wow! Great shot!" he laughed. "Who's up for sledding?"

Some of the pixies decided to play in (and nibble on) a gingerbread house that Elsie had made for them.

The rest all trudged to the edge of the hill dragging little walnut shell sleds. Soon they were sliding down the smooth white slope. High cries of "Wheeee!" filled the air.

Pooka watched until he felt a tiny tug on his fur. He looked down at Thistle. "Here's one for you," she said. The sprite showed him the bottom half of a large crockery bowl. Pooka recognized it as one of Elsie's that he'd accidentally broken. The pixies had rescued it from the trash. They'd filed the edges smooth, then drilled a little hole in one side and attached a handle made from a farmwife's "lost" ribbon. The cat was thrilled!

"Thanks, Thistle!"

"I thought you might like to join in," she smiled with a shrug of her dainty shoulder.

Berry suddenly appeared at Thistle's side. "It's from All of Us!" she told him with a sharp dig to Thistle's ribs. "I thought of it!" snapped Thistle. The two fairies glared at each other.

Pooka, however, had already dragged the bowl to the edge of the moonlit hill. He'd scarcely situated his rump and paws inside before it began its slippery descent. Within moments, he was streaking down the hill, the cold air stinging his nose and whizzing past his ears. His eyes bugged out and his heart beat fast. "I'm going to die," he thought. But as he neared the meadow, the bowl slowed and dumped him gently at the base of the hill.

He sat up in the snow with a dazed expression. "That was GREAT!" he cried. He grabbed the ribbon in his mouth and dragged the bowl back up the hill for another "go". And after that – another...and another... Eventually, he learned that by leaning one way or the other, he could steer around the pixies in their walnut sleds instead of running over them.

The ting-a-ling of a tiny bell was heard over their giggles and laughter. The wee folk immediately abandoned their sleds and hurried up the hill toward the sound.

The little cat was confused. "What's going on?" he asked.

"It's Time for the Feast!" one of the fairies answered as she flew past him.

Pooka dashed up the hill along with the others. Reaching the grove at the hilltop, he skidded to a halt. What a sight awaited him!

Hundreds of fairy lanterns glowed from the branches of the trees. Below, toadstool chairs and tiny twig thrones were lined up along dozens of birch bark tables all piled high with platters of seed cakes and honey buns, acorn bowls of soups and puddings and pitchers of fresh sweet milk. The fairies and elves scrambled into the chairs and Pooka's tummy rumbled. All that exercise had made him hungry!

Bracken, the elf, guided him to the head of one of the tables and brought him a teensy bowl of pudding. One lap of Pooka's tongue emptied the bowl. Berry presented him with a dried leaf platter of seed cakes, but when he tried to lick them up, even the leaf stuck to his tongue. It took him forever to spit it out! Thistle sighed. "Maybe you should just eat the rest of the gingerbread house," she suggested.

All the while, from the shadows under the stars, little musicians played airy tunes on instruments few humans have ever heard.

The feasting wound to a close and there was a brief lull until an elder elf with a long beard stood and announced, "It is the Sun's Birthday!" He took a sip of ginger beer and cleared his throat before continuing: "Our New Born Sun shall grow, bringing warmth to the Earth and the green creatures we care for and who give us Life in return. We celebrate this Grand Occasion with lights and song, with games and feasting and…." He paused. The pixies all held their breath. Finally he yelled, "…and PRESENTS!" Everyone cheered. Some of the younger fairies flew into the air and wheeled summersaults in their excitement.

A silvery gauze curtain in the corner of the setting was drawn back to reveal a young evergreen tree. Pooka recognized it as the one he and Elsie had filled a few days ago with treats for the birds. Besides the orange halves filled with seeds and the popcorn and cranberry garlands, it was now decked with golden acorns and walnuts, sprigs of red berry clusters and covered with tiny glowing fairy lights. Beneath, it was piled with presents – just like his and Elsie's tree back at the cottage.

Bramble, one of the smallest fairies, and Nutkin, one of the youngest elves, came forward to disperse the Solstice Treasures. The air was soon filled with "Ooohs" and "Ahhs" as the little people unveiled their gifts.

Pooka watched and purred, thinking of the catnip mouse that awaited him beneath his own tree in the morning.

Suddenly, Thistle and Berry were before him. Between them, they cradled a package.

"This is for YOU," announced Thistle.

"From ALL of us," added Berry.

The fairies and elves fell silent as the little cat (with the help of Berry and Thistle) opened the package. Inside was an exquisite, tiny, brass bell.

The elder elf with the long beard stepped forward. "Witch Cat," he said in a Very Important Voice. "We of the Smaller Kingdoms acknowledge you as a Very Special Friend. Wherefore we present you with this Bell. You have only to ring it, and we shall hear your call throughout the Forest." He cleared his throat with a loud "Ahem" and continued very quickly and quietly as though he was speaking into his beard: "We don't promise to answer, but we will hear it!" More loudly, he said: "And This, Mr. WitchCat, is our gift to You!" He puffed on his pipe and waited…

Pooka tapped the bell with his paw. It gave a faint, sweet tinkle. He purred proudly. "Thank you – All of you!" he said.

"Yes! Well then…A Very Merry Solstice to All!"

The pixies cheered and began talking excitedly amongst themselves. Thistle hugged Pooka's nose. "This is a Very Special Gift!" she whispered.

The elder elf tapped his pipe on a nearby pebble, refilled it and then lit it again. He took a few puffs before gesturing for the crowd to quiet down.

"It is almost time for the Sun to Rise!" he announced.

The fairies and elves immediately quieted and in silence trooped toward the edge of the hill facing the east.

As Pooka followed, his ears suddenly picked up the sound of footsteps crunching through the snow a little lower on the hill. Elsie!

Abandoning the fairies, he raced toward her.

"There you are!" she laughed. "Where were you? Out celebrating with the Pixies?"

He skidded to a halt in front of her. "How'd you know?" he asked.

Elsie winked and grinned. "Call it a hunch. Next time though, shut the window? I was freezing all night!"

Pooka promised he would, but you know, I know and Elsie knew that cats may open doors and windows, but they never, ever close them!

The witch set her picnic basket on the snow and spread out her blankets.

Pooka lapped up a mug of her special hot, spiced milk and nibbled some gingerbread (while carefully avoiding the raisins). Then, his tummy warm and full, he curled up in the thick, soft quilt she'd brought for him. For some reason, the little cat couldn't stop yawning!

"Pooka! Stay awake!" Elsie nudged him. "The Sun's about to rise!"

The cat forced his eyes open and stared at the faintly growing pink and gold light on the horizon. But it was no use. The Sun rose and was greeted with cheers from humans, animals and pixies alike - all except one very tired little black kitty. Pooka slept right through it!

Yule is the Sun's birthday! How do you celebrate when it's your birthday? One way is by making a wish, then blowing out the candles on your cake. Elsie has a special Yule candle that is only lit on the Winter Solstice. The rest of the year, it is carefully packed away with the rest of her decorations.

To make a Yule candle, you will need to get a fairly big candle. It can be red or white. Take a big nail or other pointy object and carve sun symbols into the candle. Make the parts you carve out about 1/8 of an inch deep. Take your time and do a good job. Think about the sun, how happy it makes you feel, how good its warmth is on your skin and all the things we need it for as you're carving.

In a small bowl or electric blender, crumble some mistletoe (a "sun" herb) into tiny bits. Then, mix the bits of mistletoe with gold glitter.

Put glue in the symbols you carved on the candle and fill the designs with the crumbled mistletoe and glitter. Let it dry. You now have a special Yule candle.

Some Sun Symbols:

A Birthday Ritual for the Sun

On your altar or a small table, place pinecones, small evergreen boughs, bay leaves, apples and other natural decorations of the season. Besides these, have a bell, some pine incense burning and your Yule candle.

Ring the Bell and say:

> *Hear the bell that I have rung*
> *Solstice Time has now begun*
> *Happy Birthday, baby Sun!*

Light the Yule candle and say:

> *Soon the dark will go away*
> *Because the Light is born this day.*

Sing the birthday song:

> *Happy Birthday to you, Happy Birthday to you*
> *Happy Birthday, dear Sun! Happy Birthday to you!*

Make a wish for the Sun to grow stronger as each day ahead moves toward Spring, and then blow out the candle and say: *Blessed Be!*

The Storybook Chair

Sharing the Holiday

Snow crunched under Elsie's boots as she trudged through the streets of the village. Behind her, Pooka padded, his own paws silent as he trotted on the ice. The little cat, however, was very noisy and vocal. The Yule season was upon them and he was excited!

"I hear bells coming from the church. Is that to announce Sacred Time?"

"Yes," said Elsie.

He spotted an evergreen wreath on a red door. "Elsie, Look! The Circle of Life!"

Elsie smiled over her shoulder and continued walking.

Pooka saw a pine tree in a window. Its branches glowed with tiny lights.

"Elsie, little Sun symbols! The Light is born again to the Earth!"

"Yes, it is," said Elsie. She kept walking. Pooka trotted behind her, his little head swiveling back and forth as he took in the festive sights and sounds. The village was crowded with shoppers all rushing about with happy expressions on their faces and their arms filled with packages. He could feel the sparkle of magic in the air!

As they passed the bakery, Elsie almost bumped into an elderly woman just coming out. "I'm so sorry, Miss Epstein!" The girl stooped to pick up the bag her friend had dropped.

"No harm done," smiled the town's librarian. "By the way, that book on beekeeping you asked for is in."

Elsie grinned. "Thank you! I'll stop by the library on my way home. Here's your bag and have a merry Christmas."

"And a happy Yule to you, my dear," said Miss Epstein.

The two parted and Elsie resumed making her way toward the pharmacy. Pooka trotted after her but he was quiet now and his furry little brain was puzzling over something.

When Elsie delivered her lavender lotion and comfrey salve to the pharmacist, he heard the curious phrase again.

"Merry Christmas, Mr. Ambercromby!"

"Thank you. And you have a wonderful Yule, little one," beamed the kindly shop-owner.

Elsie got her book from the library and they headed back home. Now that Pooka was listening, he heard the same words being echoed everywhere. "Merry Christmas!"

As they left the village and entered the forest path leading back to their cottage, he finally asked, "Why do you say Merry Christmas to people? The holiday's called Yule!"

"Because most of the people in the village are Christians," said Elsie. "And Christians celebrate Christmas at this time."

"What's Christmas?" asked the cat.

"That's when they celebrate the birth of the son of their God."

"Well, we celebrate the birth of the sun. Isn't that the same thing?"

"Yes and no," said Elsie.

"Then how come the village is filled with all those Yule symbols?" demanded Pooka. "I mean the lights, the bells, the presents everyone was buying. The mistletoe and holly and the wreaths on the doors – those are all pagan!"

Elsie paused, then tucked her cloak beneath her and sat on a snow bank under a tree. Pooka jumped in her lap.

"Long, long ago," said Elsie, "Everyone was pagan. And they all loved the Winter Solstice celebration – just as you and I do today. When a new religion came along, Christianity, the people who changed over to it didn't want to give up the fun of the old ways. So they decided to use the birthday of the sun as the birthday of their God's son too. Sort of like one big birthday party! They kept the old customs and symbols and just gave them a slightly different meaning."

Pooka thought about this for a few minutes as he snuggled against Elsie's warm tummy.

Elsie looked down at him. "My bottom's getting cold," she said. "Can we go now?"

"Okay," said Pooka. He hopped down and scampered ahead of her along the path.

As they opened the garden gate, he looked with new awareness at the round wreath of evergreens on Elsie's front door. Inside the cottage, Elsie stomped the snow off her boots and Pooka paused at the entrance to the parlor. He could smell apples and sweet spices and the pine scent of the little tree in the corner. The lights on the tree twinkled and decorations danced on its boughs. Beneath it, gay packages were filled with surprises to be discovered on Yule morning.

Elsie was hanging up her cloak as he turned to her and said: "You know what? I'm glad we can share our Yule customs with the villagers. I'd really hate for them to miss out on all this Wonderfulness!"

The little witch smiled. "Yeah, me too. By the way, Pooks, did you know you were standing under the mistletoe?" She scooped the cat up and planted a kiss on his nose. "Happy Yule!" said Elsie.

Imbolc

Imbolc means "in the belly". Even though it is still winter, spring is coming and, all over the world, new life is already growing in the bellies of mother animals. Deep within the belly of mother nature, below the snow and frozen Earth, new life is stirring there also.

The Storybook Chair

Pooka's Patience

The herb garden along the side of Elsie's little cottage was covered in white. A thin layer of white snow blanketed the ground, frosted the roof and lay along the bare branches of the old oak tree. In the middle of all this white sat a small black cat.

Pooka had on the paw-covers he'd received from Elsie last Yule – but these didn't keep his bottom from getting cold as he sat and stared at the frozen ground.

The night before, he and his witch, Elsie, had done an Imbolc ritual. Elsie had said afterward that now the earth would warm and things would begin to grow. So Pooka had parked himself in front of where the catnip had been last year – where he knew that it would come up again this year - and now he was waiting.

A flurry of black feathers landed next to him and Edgar peered with solemn gray eyes at the ground in front of Pooka. Then the crow cocked his head and asked "What'cha doing?"

"I'm waiting," replied the little cat.

"Uh huh," Edgar bobbed his head in agreement. "What for?"

"For the catnip to grow."

Edgar peered more closely. "Don't see it." He pecked at the snow with his beak and looked again. "Still don't see it," he announced.

Pooka loftily informed the crow: "Elsie said I must be Patient. But we did an Imbolc ritual last night so the green things will grow now." He resumed staring and being "Patient".

Edgar looked at his friend. Normally he thought Pooka one of the smartest creatures around (besides Elsie). He suddenly had his doubts.

"Okay…" he said. "Bet you freeze your bottom off!" And with a loud caw-caw of laughter, he lifted his wings and flew off over the trees. Pooka could hear him still laughing about a mile away.

The little cat shifted his bottom and went back to waiting.

Before long there was another flutter of wings – this time tiny and iridescent and right in front of his nose. Pooka jerked back his head and saw Thistle, the fairy, hovering before him. Her small fists were planted on her hips as she examined him.

"Are you in trouble again?" she asked.

"No."

"Then why is Elsie making you sit out here?"

"She's not "making" me," Pooka told her indignantly. "I choose to!"

Thistle's eyebrows shot up almost right off her face. "Why?"

"I'm waiting for the catnip to grow," explained Pooka – again.

Thistle folded her arms and looked at him. "It's too early," she said.

"No it's not. Elsie did an Imbolc ritual last night so now the green things will grow." The little cat was getting tired of explaining this.

"Overnight?" squeaked Thistle. "You think that's how it works?" She threw back her head in a peal of laughter.

Pooka's feelings were decidedly ruffled. Besides, he had much more faith in Elsie, his witch, than in some stupid old fairy!

"Elsie said the green things would grow," he insisted. "Catnip is a green thing."

"Yes," chirped Thistle, "but she didn't mean right now today!" The fairy dug an elbow in Pooka's ribs and winked. "Bet your bottom's getting cold, eh?"

Pooka didn't like being reminded. He growled.

Thistle left, still giggling.

A little while later, Mrs. Gilroy came up the path to the cottage and knocked on the door. Elsie opened it, smiling.

"I've come for more of that eucalyptus oil and some of your tea for coughs," the woman said. "All my kids are down with a cold. By the way, why's your silly cat sitting in the yard staring at the ground like that? You'd think his bottom would be froze solid!"

Elsie craned her neck around the door, looking over toward the herb garden. "So that's where he got off to," she muttered and then added, "Come in. I'll get your tea and eucalyptus oil."

Mrs. Gilroy disappeared inside the cottage and Pooka sat there, thoroughly disgruntled. He realized he couldn't feel his bottom anymore. He shifted position again.

As Mrs. Gilroy left, clutching her packets of herbs and oils, she looked at him and shook her head.

Pooka hoped she'd trip. He was getting very tired of people worrying about the temperature of his bottom and the catnip still wasn't growing! He dug at the ground with a paw. Nothing. Just wet dirt and snow. He sighed, shifted his bottom once more, and went back to being Patient.

Pretty soon a shadow fell over him and he glanced up to see Elsie standing there.

"Don't ask what I'm doing," he sighed.

She crouched down alongside him. "I know what you're doing," she said. "You're waiting for the catnip to grow."

"Yes!" cried Pooka, amazed. How had she known?

She smiled at the surprise on his face. "This is where it grew last year."

"Yes!" the little cat said. "So that means it will be here again this year, right? I am in the right spot? It didn't move?"

Elsie laughed. "You're in the right spot," she said. "But, Pooks, Nature doesn't happen overnight. She likes to take her time." The little witch screwed up her face and thought for a minute. "Tell you what – maybe we can hurry Her along a bit."

Pooka perked right up. "How?" he asked.

"Like this," and Elsie smacked her hand on the ground three times - like she was knocking on a door. "WAKE UP, Mother!" she yelled down.

Pooka stared at her.

"That ought to do it," the witch grinned as she dusted her hands off and stood up. "But don't forget, Mother Nature has been sleeping all winter. She needs time to stretch and get Her juices flowing. Check back in about a week - after the full moon." Elsie winked at the cat and headed back to the cottage.

A week? Pooka blinked after her retreating figure. A whole week? He wasn't going to sit out here all that time! With a plaintive meow, he sprang to his paws. He'd intended to race after her, but immediately discovered that not just his bottom was frozen – his hind legs were stiff too! He settled for an ungainly hobble.

A week later he was back in the same spot. Elsie, Thistle and Edgar were all gathered around him. Pooka looked at the thin layer of frost still covering the ground. Was it his imagination or did he see a glimmer of green underneath?

Edgar hopped over and pecked at the ice with his beak, then Elsie gently brushed the frozen bits away with her broom. They all bent over, held their breath and looked.

There it was! Tiny little gray-green leaves in a tight rosette poking through the ground!

Pooka sprang into the air. "Hurray!" he shouted.

Edgar cawed and flew in low circles. Elsie clapped her hands in delight and laughed, "Blessed be!" and Thistle sprinkled the baby leaflets with Fairy Dust to help them grow.

The little witch scooped up her celebrating cat and kissed him. "I hope you understand now. Just because you do a spell or ritual doesn't mean things are going to happen right away. Nature has Her own rhythm. We can help Her, but She's still the Boss."

Pooka tried to understand the difference…but all he could think about was that the catnip was growing and his bottom was warm!

THE LITTLE KITCHEN WITCH

Imbolc has always been closely associated with cows, butter, milk & cheese. It is traditional to leave bread and fresh butter on your windowsill or just outside the door for the goddess Brigid on the eve of Imbolc. (Don't forget to leave a bit of hay or grass for the fairy cow that travels with her!) I'll bet it would particularly please the goddess if you made the butter for her yourself. It's not difficult to do:

Set a carton of heavy whipping cream out at room temperature for about 12 to 20 hours. You want it to get sour because that will make your butter taste better.

Then, pour the room temperature cream into a jar til it's about half full. Put the lid on nice and tight. Play some music and dance around the house shaking the jar in time to the music. (You don't want to shake it too fast) It would be nice to have a friend or a brother or sister help you because it's going to take about 20 to 30 minutes for the butter to form.

You'll see little pellets of solid butter develop and separate from the milky part. When it seems like no more are forming, drain off the buttermilk part (you can use that to make buttermilk pancakes or biscuits). Use a spatula or flat wooden spoon to press the butter and work out any remaining buttermilk, then rinse it in cold water.

Now you add a bit of salt – just a pinch or two – and mix it in really good. Then put it in the refrigerator to cool and harden up a bit.

The Storybook Chair

Edgar's Secret

"*E*dgar sure has been acting strange lately," muttered Elsie.

"Huh?" Pooka looked up from his breakfast bowl and licked his whiskers.

Elsie was standing at the kitchen window gazing out after the large crow that had just left. "That's his third piece of chicken," she said. "And he hasn't eaten any of them. He just grabs one, flies off and then comes back for more. He did the same thing yesterday."

"He likes to stash food around for later," Pooka said.

Elsie nodded. "Yes, I know. But not until he's eaten enough to fill him up now." The little witch folded her arms across her apron and turned away from the window. "Something's up, Pooks. I can feel it. Think you can find out what it is?"

Pooka rubbed against her ankles. "I'll try," he said. "Right after my nap." (As every cat knows, naps are a top priority!) He stretched and yawned, then curled up in the basket that Elsie kept next to the nice warm stove.

A short while later, he was woken by the soft rustle of feathers at the window. He slit one eye open in time to see Edgar land and look furtively around the kitchen. Elsie was off working in her herb room and, except for the "sleeping" cat, the kitchen was empty. The crow hopped along the counter until he came to an old crock that Elsie had filled with fresh oatmeal cookies. A moment later, he launched away again from the open window and took to the sky, this time with a cookie in his beak. Pooka bounded through the window after him.

The ground was cold on Pooka's paws and partially melted mounds of crusty snow were piled against tree trunks and bushes. The sun had shone brightly on Imbolc a few days ago, but Elsie had insisted that another storm was coming. Pooka noticed the dark gray clouds gathering in the sky. A gust of wind cut through the cat's fur. It looked like Elsie was right – as usual. Pooka shivered. It was easy to keep the crow in sight, since most of the tree branches in the forest were still bare and it wasn't long before Edgar landed on one of them that bordered Farmer Gillis's land. His gray eyes glanced around sharply and Pooka dove for cover under a holly bush. He then saw Edgar swoop down and hop-skip towards a small shed that stood in the middle of the Gillis wheat field. Belly low to the ground, the cat slunk after him. Edgar disappeared inside the shed and then reappeared a moment later and took to the air again – without the cookie! Rather than chase the bird and demand to know what he was up to, Pooka decided to look in the shed. Gathering his courage, he crept closer. He didn't hear anything. He couldn't smell anything either over the sharp scents of the metal, grease and gasoline from farming equipment. He reached the door and peered into the darkness beyond.

Two green eyes stared back at him!

Blessed Be! Pooka hissed and his paws left the ground. He did a backwards summersault and landed with his fur poking straight out from his body. Cautiously (and Very Bravely) he slowly stuck his nose into the darkness again. The green eyes were still there, hovering in the darkness and a voice growled: "Back away from the cookie! It's MINE!" Pooka backed.

"I don't want your cookie," he said. "I just want to know who and what you are!"

The green eyes floated closer to his face and he could almost make out a nose. "Who are you?" asked the voice.

"My name's Pooka. Now it's your turn!" He heard a sigh and the eyes came even closer, followed by the brown tabby-striped face of another cat. As she stepped out into the weak light of the sun, he could see that her face and legs looked painfully thin but her belly looked like his own after a Mabon Feast!

She dipped her head shyly. "My name is Sarah."

Pooka was astounded! "What are you doing here?" he asked. "And why is Edgar bringing you food?"

Sarah studied him carefully for a moment before answering. Finally she said, "The crow is bringing me food because I am starving. My family moved away and left me. They thought I could take care of myself and didn't need them."

Pooka looked at her belly. He couldn't help say: "You don't look like you're starving."

Sarah sat and primly licked the fur on her tummy. "Well I am," she said. "The roundness you see isn't food. It's the baby kittens I'm growing inside me."

Pooka's eyes bugged open. Babies? He watched as Sarah retreated back into the darkness of the tool shed and carefully munched on her cookie. He knew he had to do something!

"You'd better come with me," he said. "Elsie and I will take care of you."

"Who's Elsie?" she asked. "And why should this Elsie want to care for me when my own people have abandoned me?"

"Elsie's a witch!" Pooka told her proudly. "And witches are healers. Don't worry. You and your babies will be safe with us."

So Sarah followed Pooka across the farmlands and through the woods toward Elsie's cottage. Several times they had to stop and rest for Sarah's tummy was heavy and her legs were still weak from being hungry for so long. But eventually, around dusk when the sun was slipping away, they made it. The light from within the cottage shone through the windows giving off a warm, welcoming glow in the cold gray twilight.

Pooka sprang to the ledge of the kitchen window that Elsie had left cracked open for him. She was at the stove and turned in surprise.

"Pooks! Where've you been?"

The cat's chest puffed out in triumph. "Solving the Edgar mystery," he told her. "And I brought someone home with me!" He stepped aside to reveal the shy little tabby cat behind him.

Elsie took in Sarah's story with one glance. She nodded and said, " I had a hunch..." A hearty stew was ladled into bowls and placed on the rug in front of the stove. It was followed by warmed, sweet cream.

Afterward, Sarah curled up in Pooka's basket by the stove and promptly fell asleep, snoring loudly. Pooka didn't mind. At night, he slept with Elsie anyway.

Over the next few days, Sarah spent most of her time just eating and sleeping. At first, during meals, Edgar would still hop over to her with bits of chicken or bread in his beak. Eventually, he realized there was no longer any need for him to share his dinner.

Before long, Sarah felt strong enough to move about more and even enjoy a gentle game of "kill the catnip mouse" with Pooka. They were in the parlor one morning batting the felt mouse around and taking turns pouncing on it when Sarah suddenly stopped and began furiously licking her side.

"I have to go now!" she said, and trotted quickly towards the kitchen.

Pooka was annoyed. The game had just been getting fun! "But you just ate!" he objected. "Don't tell me you're hungry again already?"

"Not hunger," Sarah gasped and trotted even faster.

Pooka panicked! Babies? He galloped after her calling: "Elsie! Elsie!"

The little witch's feet beat a tattoo down the wooden stairs to the kitchen. Pooka dashed around madly. "What do we do?" he meowed. "What do we do?"

Elsie smiled and picked him up. "Nothing," she said. "We let Sarah and the Goddess do their jobs. Together they'll bring the new souls back from The Other Side."

And that's what happened. How it happened is a Deep Mystery that only Mothers know. Afterward, Sarah was very tired but purring happily. Four little kittens were lined up at her side drinking the sweet milk that had developed in her body just for them. She licked their silky faces with her tongue and snuggled them against the warm fur of her belly.

Elsie hugged Pooka who purred back at her. No words were necessary. The tiny, squirming, fur covered bodies attached to a purring Sarah said it all.

Sarah and her children found a permanent home in Farmer Gillis's barn. They kept the mice at bay and made sure the gophers living at the edges of his fields minded their manners. And Elsie and Pooka never forgot that cold February morning when four tiny miracles happened in the kitchen of the cottage.

Elsie's HERB GARDEN

Pooka woke from his nap and sniffed the air. Yule was over, but he could swear he smelled gingerbread! The little cat leaped down from his perch in the windowsill and padded into the kitchen. His eyes scanned the countertops and table but he didn't see any plates of warm, spicy, sweet bread. Maybe it was still in the oven? He sauntered over, but could tell instantly that the oven was cold. Puzzled, he sat down in the middle of the floor and scratched behind his ear with a back paw.

Elsie was standing at the counter brewing a cup of tea.

"I give up," said Pooka.

Elsie turned and raised an eyebrow. "Eh?" she asked.

"Where's the gingerbread I'm smelling?" demanded Pooka.

Elsie lifted her teacup. "Here it is," she told him.

Pooka fixed her with a cat stare. "Right!" he said.

He jumped up on the counter and stuck his nose in the cup then jerked back. He was more confused than ever. There was nothing in the cup but tea! The look on his face must have been pretty funny because the little witch giggled.

"The 'ginger' part of gingerbread is an herb," she told him. "That's what you smell."

"But why are you drinking the herb instead of making me some yummy cake out of it?" asked Pooka.

Elsie grimaced. "Because I ate too many Yule sweets and now my tummy's upset."

"And the ginger will help your tummy?"

The witch nodded and took a sip from the cup. "Ginger's one of the best things in the world when you feel nauseous," she said.

"Nauseous…you mean…" Pooka's eyes bugged out. "You're not going to throw up are you?" The cat was horrified. Throwing up was messy and yucky! What if some of it got on his fur? Ewwe!

He quickly backed out of the way. Then, still not satisfied that he was out of range, he jumped down from the counter and ran to the other side of the kitchen. He stood warily in the doorway and suggested she have some more ginger tea – Fast!

Elsie just smiled, settled herself in the rocking chair and continued sipping. She knew she'd feel better soon, but in the meantime it was fun to watch Pooka panic.

Ginger

Ginger's good for other things besides upset tummies and making gingerbread. It also helps when you have gas. And on a cold winter day when you've been out playing and your fingers and toes are frozen, nothing will warm you up faster than a cup of ginger tea with honey! Grandmas and Grandpas often find that ginger will relieve the pain in their joints caused by arthritis and it's a good tea for anyone to drink when they have a cold.

By the way, when you're making a tea from ginger, the fresh roots from the grocery store or your garden work best, but for baking or incense, use the powdered stuff.

Magically, ginger is a "catalyst" - one of those herbs you can add to other herbs to shake them up, kick them in the fanny and make them work faster and better. So if you were making an incense to help you attract more friends, you might add a little bit of powdered ginger to get faster results. By itself, ginger is often used for joy, luck and money. (Dragons love ginger!)

Ginger is a beautiful plant and so much fun to grow. You can even start right now!

Go to the grocery store and find a smooth, shiny ginger root with lots of little buds or "eyes" like you've seen on a potato.

When you get it home, stick 3 or 4 toothpicks in the side of the root to help you suspend it halfway into a jar or drinking glass. Fill the jar with water until the bottom third of the root is submerged. Put it in a warm place in your home and check it every day to see if it needs more water.

Very soon you will see little thread like roots start growing.

When they get about an inch long, take the toothpicks out and plant it flat side down in a pot of soil. You'll need to use a good, rich potting soil and a pot that's about 14 inches across and 12 inches deep. Cover it with another inch of soil.

Put the pot in a warm sunny window and keep the soil damp.

You can put your ginger plant outside on a patio or under a tree when the weather is warm but be sure to give it plenty of water. Ginger gets thirsty!

Elsie's Tummy Trouble Tea

¼ inch slice of fresh Ginger root
1 Star anise
a small piece of cinnamon stick

Simmer these with a cup of water for about 5 minutes in a closed cauldron or other container. Then turn off the fire and add: 1 tsp mint

Cover it again and let it sit another 5 minutes before straining the herbs out. Then, sip it very slowly.

The Storybook Chair

Candle Magic

*T*he snow was feeling lazy. It took its time as it floated from the sky and enjoyed the sights along the way before coming to rest in a pile against the cottage.

Inside the cottage was warm and dry – but no less lazy. Everyone was lazy, that is, except for Elsie. On this Imbolc eve, she was bustling about like a little black bee in spring. Pots bubbled on the stove in the kitchen and cheese bread was baking in the oven. In the parlor, her great cauldron stood upon the hearth where a cheery fire crackled, and freshly dipped candles of every hue hung cooling on racks.

The little witch darted back and forth between the two rooms, alternately stirring pots and dipping candles. Pooka was parked in Elsie's chair, paws tucked into his chest. Thistle the fairy lay next to him, idly braiding his whiskers.

They were both bored!

Finally, Pooka asked: "How come you're making so many candles, Elsie?"

The witch barely paused as she told him: "Tomorrow's Imbolc – also known as Candlemas. It's time to make and bless our candles for the year!"

Thistle commented approvingly, "So many pretty colors."

"Yes," nodded Elsie. "And each of them represents something."

Pooka yawned and his whiskers sprang back into place. "They do?" he asked. "Like what?"

Elsie actually stood still for a moment as she considered his question. "Well," she said, "This pink one is for friendship and the yellow one's for happiness."

Thistle flew to the top of the rack. "What about this one?" she asked pointing to a green candle. "Growing things?"

The witch nodded. "That's right."

Pooka wanted to know what the brown candle was for. Elsie smiled. "Anything to do with the earth, home, business," she said. "In this case, it represents our cottage."

"And blue?" asked Thistle. (She liked the color blue.)

"Blue represents peace so, for instance, if you burn it next to a brown candle, it would create a spell for a peaceful home."

After the witch had left the room to check on her bread, Thistle fluttered back to Pooka and snuggled against his warm tummy. "So, Pooks," she asked, "What's your color wish for this year?"

Pooka's brow furrowed as he thought.

"I dunno," he said. "Pink, maybe? Friends are important. I like my friends."

"Especially ME," Thistle grinned up at him.

"I also like the idea of our home being peaceful and happy."

Thistle nodded sleepily. "Okay, that's brown and blue. What about Green Things growing?" she added.

"Yeah, like my catnip," he said.

Suddenly they sat up and looked at each other.

"Are you thinking what I'm thinking?" asked the fairy.

A short while later, Elsie bustled back into the parlor. "Blessed Be!" she exclaimed. "What's this?"

On the warm hearth lay the candles she'd hung - all melted and molded together into one glorious glop - their little wicks poking out at one end like porcupine quills.

"We made one big candle," said Pooka proudly.

"Yeah, 'cause we want it all!" said Thistle throwing her little arms open wide. "Friends, home, happiness…"

"…and catnip," added Pooka. "Can we bless our candle tomorrow during the Imbolc ritual? Please, Elsie?" he asked.

"Just look how pretty it is!" cried Thistle.

Elsie looked at the melted rainbow mess on her hearth, shook her head and smiled. "Of course," she said. "Why not?"

Imbolc is the time for cleaning and blessing everything – even ourselves! Pooka uses his tongue but Witches, both big and little, will often use the bathtub for this. Now, hang on … we're not talking about a regular bath here. This is a special Purification Bath, and I think you'll like it!

You will need some old nylons or tights that are okay to cut up. Cut the legs off about 6 inches from the toe. Save the bottom part (where the foot goes) and throw the rest away. You will now have two "bags" that you can fill with:

"Elsie's Purification Bath Blend"

In a big bowl, mix together 1 cup of salt (Kosher Salt from the grocery store works good) and 2 cups of plain, uncooked oatmeal.

Add a 1/2 cup of herbs. Some good purification herbs to choose from are Vervain, Rosemary, Hyssop, Yarrow, Eucalyptus, Lavender, Bay, Basil and Sage. (You can add more than one kind of herb.) Mix it all up and then add about 9 drops of blue food coloring (blue is for spirit) and about 21 drops of oil. Frankincense, sandalwood, lavender, eucalyptus, lemongrass, rosemary, are all good choices.

Finally, mix in ½ cup of powdered dried milk. Besides being "special" to Imbolc and the moon, the milk leaves your skin all soft and nice.

Put about one cup of the mixture in one of the bags and close the opening with a rubber band. (Store the rest away in a jar along with the other bag for next time.)

Elsie likes to take her special bath by candlelight. You might want to ask your parent if that's okay.

Toss the bag of Purification Blend into the water and, with your finger, draw a spiral in the air over the tub beginning in the center and spiraling outward. Then, when you get in, swish the bag around and squeeze it underwater with your hands, seeing the magic spreading through the water as you do. You can even use it as a washcloth. It feels good and smells good too!

Use your magical imagination to see yourself getting sparkling clean inside as well as out.

Pooka says:

You can also carve a Pentacle on a bar of soap to use in your Purification Bath.

The Storybook Chair

Listening to the Silence

Pooka was parked on the wide ledge of the parlor window. Through the leaded glass panes he gazed out at the garden – or rather where the garden HAD been before a thick blanket of snow had draped over it the night before.

Imbolc had just passed and soon the signs of spring would appear – green buds immerging, birds twittering and windows opening wide as the days grow warmer…

But, right now, it seemed the whole world was pale and white and eerily silent.

His ears swiveled backward as he heard Elsie shuffling around in the entryway of the cottage. In the quiet that had surrounded him, her gentle movements seemed especially loud. Curious, Pooka leaped down from the ledge and went to see what she was doing.

He found the witch pulling on her thick, warm cloak and adjusting the hood.

"Where are we going?" he asked.

"I am going out into the forest to meditate," she told him.

Pooka thought about this. "It's cold out there," he pointed out.

"That's why I'm wearing my cloak."

Elsie reached for the door.

The cat dashed in front her legs, effectively barring the way.

"But why not do your meditation in here where it's nice and toasty warm?"

Elsie smiled and crouched down to stroke his head. "Pooks, have you ever noticed how the forest becomes very still at this time of year and especially right after a fresh fall of snow? While Mother Earth is sleeping, all the normal busy sounds you hear during the rest of the year are quiet. The silence is so loud you can hear it."

"And you have to go out in the freezing cold to meditate on this?" he asked.

Elsie nodded.

"Alright," the little cat said grudgingly. "Let's go."

Elsie's boots crunched along the snowy path over the bridge that crossed the stream and led into the forest. Pooka padded alongside. The path winded its way through naked trees and, eventually, into a clearing with a large fallen log. Elsie sat on the log, tucked her feet up and gathered her cloak around her. "Now, hear how quiet and peaceful everything is? Mother Earth is sleeping," she whispered. "Let's meditate and listen to the Silence."

The witch closed her eyes and inhaled deep slow breaths of frosty air as she began to enter a meditative state. Pooka sat next to her, tucked his paws into his chest and tried to do likewise.

After a few moments, he realized that everything was NOT silent. His sharp ears detected a faint rustling from within the hollow log. He crept quietly down, so he wouldn't disturb Elsie and moved around to have a look. Curled up inside was a rabbit!

The rabbit saw Pooka at the same time. Its startled eyes widened and then it darted out the other side of the log. Pooka immediately dashed through the log and out, giving chase. The two of them ran in circles around the clearing until the rabbit dove under a bramble hedge and disappeared.

Pooka plopped his bottom down in the snow, his tail twitching in agitation. He was very disappointed that the rabbit didn't want to play anymore!

Elsie opened one eye and glared at him. "Are you quite done?" she asked as the little cat trotted toward her.

"Just a minute," he said and paused to sharpen his claws on a nearby tree. His activity dislodged a bit of the bark and revealed a beetle that had been hibernating underneath. The beetle scurried upward in search of another hiding place and Pooka, of course, scrambled after it.

A squirrel, whose nest was overhead, immerged and loudly scolded the rambunctious cat. "My wife is pregnant and she was sleeping!" he chattered. "Don't you know you're disturbing her?"

Pooka didn't like being scolded. He decided to confront the squirrel and tell HIM to quiet down because Elsie was meditating! The cat and the squirrel chased each other around the tree, leaping from branch to branch, and arguing loudly. Piles of snow that had been resting on the branches came plummeting to the ground and one of them finally plopped right on Elsie's head! The impact sent her tumbling backward off the log where she landed with her boots sticking straight up in the air.

Pooka and the squirrel peered down at her. "Ooops," said Pooka.

"I give up!" the witch exclaimed.

Pooka scrambled back down the tree and galloped over to her.

"You mean you're all done meditating on the Silence?" he asked eagerly.

Elsie looked at the little cat and growled.

WitchCrafts

A Whimsical Magickal Broom

You can take a regular household broom and make it into a wonderful whimsical magic broom!

Here's how:

You will need sandpaper, Paints in a bunch of colors and some varnish.

Lightly rough up the finish on the handle with sandpaper. Then mark off sections of the handle with a line of black paint.

Fill in these sections with paint in various bright colors.

When this has dried, paint fun, magical symbols in each section - moons, suns, pentagrams, spirals, dollar signs for prosperity, runes… Let your magical imagination guide you.

When this dries, cover the handle with a good coat of varnish to protect it.

When you are all finished, you might want to do a

Broom Blessing

Sprinkle your broom with salt water, then swing it around you in a clockwise circle three times and say:

Blessed be this special broom,
May it bless each little room,
Sweep the yukky stuff away
And guard this house by night and day
This my will as said by me –
And as I will, so mote it be!

CPSIA information can be obtained
at www.ICGtesting.com
Printed in the USA
LVOW02s1524031216

515617LV00006B/9/P